POLAND

Poland is a hospitable and friendly
country with countless reminders
of its great past, a picturesque landscape
and outstanding natural riches.
Its folk tradition survives inmany places.
Together, these factors confirm
Poland's status as an interesting
and attractive land
for tourists.

D1443641

POLAND

Wydawnictwo PARMA® PRESS

Poland lies at the geometric centre of Europe. In the north it is washed by the waves of the Baltic Sea, while in the south it is also limited by a natural boundary in the form of the Western Carpathians, which extend from the Bieszczady Mountains, via the Tatras and Beskids, as far as the Sudetic Mountains and the picturesque Karkonosze. In the east, Poland ends at the River Bug, while in the west it is the Oder and Nysa Łużycka that form the border. Though very largely a land of plains, an average altitude of 174 m a.s.l. conceals the fact that this is a far from monotonous landscape.

The Polish coast tends to be a flat one of wide sandy beaches, though occasional cliffs rise up here and there, as at Gdynia Orłowo. There are also extensive coastal dunes, for example in the Łeba area.

As we move south from the Baltic we encounter a zone of extensive lakelands, including the Pomeranian Lakeland and the Mazurian Lake District. The landscape here is predominantly post-glacial, with a wealth of what are Poland's largest and deepest lakes set amongst morainic elevations covered in forest. Perhaps the least diverse countryside, though no less charming for that, is the plainland heart of Poland, formed by the Mazowsze (Mazovia), Wielkopolska and Silesian regions.

Still further south, the land rises steadily: first in a belt formed by the Lublin, Małopolska and Silesian Uplands. An interesting area within the second of these is that of the Kraków-Wieluń Upland with its characteristic limestone rocks, a wealth of caves and picturesque gorges. A major tourist attraction here is the Trail of the Eagles' Nests (Szlak Orlich Gniazd) with its ruins of Mediaeval castles and fortresses.

The mountains proper arise just a little further to the south. In the south-eastern corner, the gentleness of the Bieszczady Mountain peaks belies the nature of what is a heavily-forested and truly wild land. Moving west along the southern border we reach the Tatras, Poland's youngest and highest mountains, having passed through the Pieniny Range, with its famous gorge of the Dunajec.

Still further to the west the highlands continue with the Silesian Beskids. The Sudetic Mountains begin at the so-called Moravian Gate. The most interesting range within them are the Karkonosze Mountains, where the rock formations take on the strangest of shapes.

The country's biggest river, the Vistula, flows from south to north. It is one of the last big rivers in Europe to remain very largely unregulated.

The name Poland itself relates back to the Polanie tribe, a people inhabiting what is now Wielkopolska in the Early Middle Ages.

The year 966 saw Poland's conversion to Christianity with the baptism of Mieszko I, regarded as the first leader of Poland. He was succeeded by his son Bolesław the Brave, who was able to found a strong and stable state with its capital in Gniezno. His death was followed by a collapse of authority made worse by the division of the country into districts from 1138 on – a consequence of provisions in the last will and testament of Bolesław III "Wrymouth". The reunification of the country had to wait until 1320, a year which marked a highpoint in the 27-year reign of Władysław I ("the Short").

In the mid 14th century the Polish throne was occupied by King Kazimierz III ("the Great"), who was able to strengthen the country in terms of its internal security and its economic prowess. It was he who founded Poland's first university (later known as the Jagiellonian) in Kraków, and he who has gone down in history as the ruler who "found Poland in wood and left her in brick". At the same time, however, the growing strength of the Order of the Teutonic Knights left Poland cut off from its access to the Baltic, while threatening the very existence of Lithuania. This state of affairs led to the Polish-Lithuanian Union of 1385 and the subsequent rule of the Jagiellonian Dynasty. This made a promising start when a united army under Władysław Jagiełło defeated the Teutonic Knights at the Battle of Grunwald in 1410.

Economic growth continued and the power of the nobility increased. By the 16th century, Poland was something of a superpower, being Europe's largest state, and one of its richest. This was the so-called Golden Age in the country's history. It was also at this time that Zygmunt III Vasa transferred his capital from Kraków to Warsaw.

Later decades were less happy for Poland. A Cossack revolt broke out in the Ukraine, while the Swedish invasion or "Deluge" brought territorial losses and economic ruin. The country's internal stability was lost and a central authority was often lacking.

In seeking to restore statehood from all this chaos, Poles commenced with reforms in education, the economy and defence. The crowning of these efforts came with the adoption in 1791 of the very progressive Constitution of May 3rd, Europe's first, and only the second in the world after that of the United States.

Alas, this national reconciliation came too late. The three partitions of 1772, 1793 and 1795 saw Poland divided between the Russian, Prussian and Austrian Empires. The result was the country's disappearance from the map of Europe for 123 years.

Poles launched uprisings again and again, but it was only in 1918 – as the disasters of the First World War combined with revolution to bring the three partitioning powers low – that Poland regained its statehood. Józef Piłsudski became leader of the reborn country on November 11th 1918 – recognised to this day as Polish Independence Day.

The freedom was shortlived. Hitler's Nazis fell upon Poland on September 1st 1939, thereby precipitating the Second World War. Polish soldiers fought on all fronts, but the War's end in 1945 did not resolve the matter of independence. Rather, the Yalta Conference left Poland firmly under the influence of the Soviet Union.

Many years of steadfast national opposition to an imposed system were ultimately to lead to the establishment of the Solidarity trade union in 1980. The mass opposition to the communist authorities it was

able to mobilise ensured that it was only a matter of time before the regime began to give way. The breakthrough year was 1989, when representatives of the opposition and the then authorities met at the "Round Table" to discuss the gradual democratisation of the country. Solidarity's leader, Lech Wałęsa, was ultimately to become President. The events begun in Poland had meanwhile exerted a far-from-trivial influence on the political situation throughout Europe.

The return of national sovereignty led Poland to seek NATO membership, which it achieved on March 12th 1999. In turn, economic development and political will allowed the country to accede to the European Union on May 1st 2004.

The Poland of today covers around 312,500 km^2. It is bounded in the West by Germany, in the south by the Czech Republic and Slovakia, and in the east by Ukraine, Belarus, Lithuania and Russia. The emblem of Poland is a crowned white eagle facing to its right, with golden beak and talons, in a red field upon a rectangular shield.

Poland has c. 40 million inhabitants, mainly of Polish nationality and very largely Roman Catholic. Their faith sustained by the first Polish Pope in history, His Holiness John Paul II. Poles do not forget the martyrs of the past, and there are many monuments and places of national remembrance. The largest of all is at Oświęcim – site of the former Auschwitz Concentration Camp.

Poland has a wealth of UNESCO World Heritage Sites including Old Kraków, the town of Zamość with its Renaissance architecture, the Wieliczka and Bochnia Salt Mines and the Białowieża National Park (which is also a Biosphere Reserve).

Poland is a hospitable and friendly country with countless reminders of its great past, a picturesque landscape and outstanding natural riches. Its folk tradition survives in many places. Together, these factors confirm Poland's status as an interesting and attractive land for tourists.

Superlatives

The largest city:	– Warsaw, the capital of Poland, on the Vistula, with c.1.7 million inhabitants and an area of around 500 km^2;
The largest voivodship (province):	– Mazowieckie (formerly Mazovia, capital Warsaw), which today covers c. 36,000 km and has more than 5 million inhabitants;
The longest river:	– the Vistula (Wisła), which has its source beneath Barania Góra in the Silesian Beskid Range and runs 1068 km to empty into the Baltic in the Gulf of Gdańsk;
The highest peak:	– the north-western summit of Rysy at 2499 m, within the High Tatras;
The lowest point:	– an altitude of 1.8 m a.s.l. in the Żuławy Wiślane (Vistula Delta) area;
The deepest lowland lake:	– the ribbon-lake Lake Hańcza in the Mazurian Lakeland, with a maximum depth of 108 m;
The deepest mountain lake:	– the cirque-lake known as Wielki Staw Polski (the Great Polish Tarn), one of the lakes in The Valley of the Five Polish Tarns (Dolina Pięciu Stawów Polskich) within the High Tatras – maximum depth 79.3 m;
The largest lake:	– the morainic lake Lake Śniardwy covering 109.7 km^2 in the Mazurian Lakeland;
The largest National Park:	– the Biebrza (Biebrzański) National Park, protecting 59,223 ha of fen and bogland unique anywhere in Europe;
The largest church:	– Poland's largest church is at Licheń Stary near Konin, a Sanctuary of Our Lady and Basilica enclosing a volume of no less than 300,700 m^3;
The largest castle:	– the Gothic-style 13th-15th century fortress of the Teutonic Knights at Malbork, an outstanding example of a Mediaeval fortification;
The best-known sanctuary:	– that of the Virgin Mary with its miraculous likeness of the Black Madonna, on the Jasna Góra hill in Częstochowa;
The longest market square:	– the 400-metre cobbled example in Pułtusk;
The oldest place of learning:	– Kraków's Jagiellonian University established in 1364;
The oldest town:	– Kalisz, referred to as Kalisia in the 2nd century AD by Ptolemy;
The most unusual residence:	– the Krzyżtopór castle which boasted – before its destruction – as many windows as there are days in the year, as many rooms as there are weeks, as many halls as there are months and as many towers as there are quarters. The ceiling of one hall formed the floor of an aquarium with fish;
The oldest entry in Polish:	– "Day, ut ia pobrusa, a ti poziwai" ("Give it here, I'll turn it and you rest"), in the "Book of Henryków" from 1270

GDAŃSK is an old Hanseatic town whose major development occurred in the 15th to 18th centuries, when it was the wealthiest city in the Republic. Gdańsk is a historic port city and one of the most outstanding complexes of heritage buildings in Poland. To be seen here is a panorama of the historical Main Town (Główne Miasto), with the St. Mary's (Mariacki) Church from the 14th-15th centuries – the largest place of worship in Poland.

GDAŃSK. The city's coat of arms with its lions – a decorative element of the fence around the Neptune Fountain.

GDAŃSK. The Neptune Fountain
on Długi Targ (the Long Market).

GDAŃSK. Gold Gdańsk
coins issued to
celebrate Johann III
Sobieski's visit to
the city in 1677.

GDAŃSK. The walls of the Great Council Room have
been covered with red tapestries of the same
colouring for the last three centuries.

GDAŃSK. A view of the Long Quayside
by the Motława.

GDAŃSK. The richly-decorated portal of one
of the tenement houses on Długi Targ.

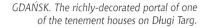

GDYNIA. Located in Kościuszki Square, the residential tower blocks known as the Sea Towers have become a new symbol of the city in the time since their completion in 2010.

SOPOT is the lying between Gdańsk a. Gdynia and forming with the so-coll Trójmiasto ("Tri-City"). An attractive tour centre, it boasts sea bathing, health-res facilities and a 19th-centry pi

GDYNIA ORŁOWO with its elevated c. coastline so unsual for Polar.

GDYNIA. The ZUS (Polish Social Insurance Institution) office building, designed by the engineer Roman Piotrowski, and built in the years 1935-1936. It is regarded as a pearl of Modernism.

SOPOT. Zbigniew Jóźwik's statue of Georg Haffner, the founder of the Sopot health resort.

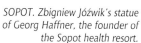

SŁOWIŃSKI NATIONAL PARK by the Baltic coast has been recognised as a Biosphere Reserve by UNESCO. Its mobile dune fields are a major attraction.

TRZĘSACZ, where we visit the famous clifftop ruins of a 14th-century church " claimed by the sea".

MIĘDZYZDROJE is a fashionable place of seaside recreation.

THE BALTIC SEA.
The seashore in Dziwnów.

An inseparable element of the seaside fauna – the ever-noisy and ever-present gulls.

SZCZECIN is a large commercial port and cent of shipbuilding on the Szczecin Lagoon. Its O Market Square boasts a 15th-century Town Ha

SZCZECIN. The ornate doorw of a tenement house on Grodzka Stree

SZCZECIN began as a Lusatian settlement 2500 years ago. It was part of the Hanseatic League from the 13th century onwards. Wały Chrobrego is a leading thoroughfare along the Oder, lined by monumental buildings from the early 20th century.

...tember 2014 brought the opening of the new ...zecin Philharmonic Hall. The slightly disturbing ...ꞵ of pointed forms has a chance of becoming ...new iconic landmark identifying the city.

SZCZECIN. The Renaissance castle of the Dukes of Pomerania is multi-winged, with two courtyards. It was rebuilt post-1945.

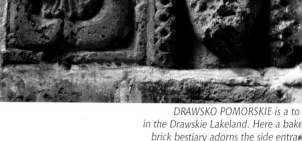

KRĄG. The castle here – erected
in the early 15th century and made
over in the Renaissance style
at the end of the 16th – was the seat
of the von Podewils family.

DRAWSKO POMORSKIE is a to
in the Drawskie Lakeland. Here a bake
brick bestiary adorns the side entra
of a 14th-century chur

TUCZNO. The castle of the Wedel family is
Mediaeval, its Renaissance-style features and
decorative sgraffito plasterwork being the results
of a mid-16th-century renovation.

KAMIEŃ POMORSKI. A section
the Baroque-style pulpit in the Got
Cathedral of the Blessed Virgin M.
and St. John the Bapt.

KAMIEŃ POMORSKI is a health resort on
the Kamieńskie Lagoon, a few kilometres inland
from the sea.This old fortified port town boasts
a late-Gothic Town Hall from the 15th-16th centuries.

ZECINEK and its 19th-century red-brick
n Hall, a characteristic Neo-Gothic
ding in the Wolności square.

STARGARD SZCZECIŃSKI is a Western
Pomeranian town with a mediaeval
architectural plan. The Gothic interior of
St Mary's Church from the late 13th century,
decorated with tiled multicoloured bricks.

BISKUPIN. The reconstruction of an early Slav settlement from the Hallstatt period. 25 centuries ago this settlement had about 1000 inhabitants!

BISKUPIN. The outdoor archaeological museum features, not only buildings and equipment, but also clothing, from far-off days.

OSTRÓW LEDNICKI. An island with an archaeological reserve, regional open-air museum and ruins of a 10th-century ducal castle.

...EZNO. In the 8th century, this was the main walled ...n of the Polanie tribe. The 14th-15th century ...hic Cathedral of the Assumption of the Virgin Mary ...St. Adalbert was the place of coronation ...ve Polish Kings.

...EZNO. The silver confessional ...t. Adalbert (St. Wojciech) ...niezno Archicathedral.

GNIEZNO. A scene from the Gniezno Doors
(the 2nd half of the 12th century) showing the arrival
of St. Adalbert in Prussia in the year 997.

POZNAŃ. In the course of rebuilding follow
wartime destruction, the Cathedral on Ost
Tumski Island in Poznań regained its Gothic fc
albeit with relict Romanesque features retair
This is one of Poland's oldest churc
and its oldest of all Basilica, a title it
enjoyed since the year S

POZNAŃ – situated on the Warta
– is the historic capital of the Wielkopolska
region. The Cathedral of Saints Peter and Paul
on Ostrów Tumski island had its origins
in the 10th century.

POZNAŃ. Bronze likenesses of two members
of Poland's Piast dynasty: Mieszko I
and Bolesław Chrobry ("the Brave"),
in the Golden Chapel at Poznań Cathedral.

POZNAŃ. The goats of the Town Hall clock
...age in butting contests daily at midday.

POZNAŃ. The Town Hall's Great Hall or Revival Hall
boasts a 16th-century caissoned ceiling which
is the work of Giovanni Battista di Quadro.

POZNAŃ. The Town Hall elevation comprises three
stories of an arcade loggia, all topped off by an attic
imitating town walls, as well as a slender tower.

POZNAŃ. A small
sculpture of a female
settler from
Bamberg, 1914.

RYDZYNA is a small historic town in the Wielkopolska region. Standing in an extensive landscaped park, the Baroque palace of the Sułkowski family dates back to the 17th and 18th centuries.

DĘBOWA ŁĘKA. A stork's nest – a typically Polish view.

RZELNO. The interior of the Church of the Holy Trinity and Blessed Virgin Mary is graced with seven Romanesque columns covered with a figurative low relief and adornments.

KÓRNIK. The original castle dating back to 1426 was extensively remodelled in the English Neo-Gothic style in the 19th century.

KOSZUTY near Środa Wielkopolska. This 18th-century manor house – today it houses the Museum of the Środa Region.

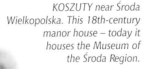

ROGALIN. The Raczyńskis' palace built in the 18th century combines Rococo and Neo-Classical features.

SZRENIAWA station. "Age of Steam" heritage along the Poznań-Wolsztyn Line.

GOSTYŃ, with its
Philippinian monastery
complex, Sanctuary to
the Virgin Mary and
17th-century church,
and well in
the viridarium.

WIELKOPOLSKI NATIONAL PARK.
On the northern shore of Góreckie Lake.

GOŁUCHÓW *boasts a 16th-century Renaissance castle remodelled in the style of the French Renaissance in the 19th century and set in picturesque English-style parkland.*

THE RACOT STUD *stable specializes in the breeding of pedigree half-breed horses with horses of the Wielkopolska region. This breed can be used for horseback riding and horse-carts, as well as for sports and recreation.*

WROCŁAW. The Racławicka panorama is a 19th century pain[...] battle scene with a circumference of 114 m and a hei[...] of 15 m. It represents the work of a great many art[...] under the direction of Wojciech Kossak and Jan Sty[...]

WROCŁAW. The characteristic Gothic Town Hall, from the 14th-15th centuries, features richly-decorated facades and a 66-metre tower.

WROCŁAW, the capital of Lower Silesia, is a historic city on the Oder which began life as a Slav settlement in the first millennium. Standing on Ostrów Tumski island is the Gothic Cathedral dedicated to St. John the Baptist.

WROCŁAW. A sculpted Madonna and Child from 1694 at the entrance to the Cathedral on Ostrów Tumski island.

WROCŁAW, the Century Hall (Hala Stulecia) is to a Max Berg design from 1913, and is now entered on UNESCO's World Heritage List.

WROCŁAW apparently boasts some 220 crossings of different kinds over the Oder and its different ramifying channels. The Grunwaldzki (former Kaiserbrücke) Bridge was put up in the years 1908-1910.

WROCŁAW. A leading example of the Silesian Baroque, the 1732 Aula Leopoldina forming part of the complex of buildings of Wrocław University.

WROCŁAW. Syzyfek the Dwarf has been shaving his stone sphere down Świdnicka Street since 2001. He was the first of the Wrocław Dwarfs, of which there are now about hundred.

KARPACZ is a holiday resort at the foot of Śnieżka mountain. The Wang church was brought here from Norway in the 19th century, though its origins go back six centuries before that.

THE KARKONOSZE form a range within the Sudetic Mountains that peak at the 1602 m Śnieżka massif. In winter they take on a particular beauty.

The rocky labyrinth at the top of Szczeliniec Wielki, the highest peak of the Stołowe Mountains (919 m asl) has an abundance of fantastic rock formations. One such formation, Małpolud (Ape man), has become the symbol of the region.

JASKINIA NIEDŹWIEDZIA (the Bear Cave) lies at the foot of Śnieżnik and is richer in dripstone features than any other cave in Poland.

ŚWIERADÓW-ZDRÓJ. The wooden promenade hall from 1899, with its stations at which the local mineral waters can be drunk.

CZERMNA near Kudowa-Zdrój. The "Chapel
Skulls" brings together the remains of the
who fell in the Silesian Wars or chole
epidemics of the 18th centu

KSIĄŻ. The well in the Castl
"Black Courtyard

THE KAMIEŃCZYK WATERFALL close to
Szklarska Poręba has three cascades
descending 27 m overall.

NRYKÓW. Silesia's most ornate choir stalls are
se examples from around 1710 in the formerly
tercian Church of the Assumption
J St. John the Baptist.

WAMBIERZYCE is a well-known
place of pilgrimage whose
Sanctuary to the Virgin Mary
led it to be called the Silesian
Jerusalem. The monumental
56-step staircase leads to the late
Baroque Church of the Visitation.

KSIĄŻ – the castle features
nearly 400 rooms in various
architectural styles.
The Baroque ballroom
from the first half of the
18th century is known as
the Maximilian Room.

KŁODZKO. The Gothic-style stone bridge over the Młynówka is considered by some to resemble a mini-version of Prague's Charles Bridge. It links Sand Island with the Old Town.

KRZESZÓW. The Baroque-style form Cistercian abbey complex first func in 1242. A famous Lenten devot of the Via Dolorosa takes pl here each ye

LEŚNA, Czocha (Tzschocha) Castle is a Gothic-Renaissance structure by Lake Leśniańskie. It was refurbished and brought back to standard by Bodo Ebhardt in the years 1909-1914.

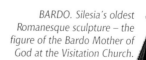

BARDO. Silesia's oldest Romanesque sculpture – the figure of the Bardo Mother of God at the Visitation Church.

DUSZNIKI-ZDRÓJ. The Museum of Papermaking has its seat in the Baroque-style papermill building.

VOR. The Evangelical Church of the Holy Ghost "Peace Church" is Early Baroque in style, d shaped like a rectangle with four levels seating. It can accommodate 6000 people.

ŚWIDNICA, Church of Peace.
Western elevation of the beautiful
half-timbered wall construction.

BRZEG. 17th-century scratchwork decoration on the elevation of the Town Hall courtyard.

BRZEG. Sculpted Renaissance-style decorative elements on the gatehouse of the Castle of the Silesian Piasts.

PACZKÓW. The Church of St John the Evangelist – an extraordinary example of a fortified building built in the mid 14th century.

NYSA. In the late 19th century the Church of St James and St Agnes became neo-Gothic in its shape and a new western porch with a decorative portal was added.

OPOLE. A sandstone epitaph for the Skopek family from 1660 forms part of the wall in the Cathedral of the Raising of the Holy Cross.

OPOLE. The Młynówka, one of the several branches of the Oder that have led locals to use the term "the Opole Venice".

MAŁUJOWICE. The Church of St James the Apostle is situated on the route of the polychromes of Brzeg. Its interior is graced with medieval paintings, which form a biblical cycle known as the Biblia Pauperum.

...SZNA, near Opole, features an eclectic-...castle from the late 19th century.

CIESZYN, on the Olza, is the capital of Cieszyn Silesia. The Market Squa[re] southern side features an eclectic building in which the so-called Dom Po[lski] was established in 1901, as a centre for Polish cultural and political [life]. Alongside is the Post Office building, as well as a statue of St. Flor[ian].

A girl from the "Śląsk" song and dance ensemble in the traditional townwear of the region known as Cieszyn (Teschen) Silesia.

CIESZYN. The 11th-century Romanesque-style rotunda dedicated to St. Nicholas is situated on the tree-covered Castle Hill. It takes the form of a circle of diameter 6.4 m.

BIELSKO-BIAŁA. The imposing Council Chamber on the first floor of the Town Hall erected in the years 1895-1897, to a design from Emanuel Rost.

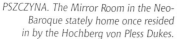

PSZCZYNA. The Mirror Room in the Neo-Baroque stately home once resided in by the Hochberg von Pless Dukes.

TARNOWSKIE GÓRY. A route 1740 m long has been made available to visitors at the Zabytkowa Kopalnia Rud Srebronośnych (Heritage Mine of Silver-Bearing Ores).

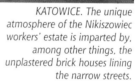

KATOWICE. The unique atmosphere of the Nikiszowiec workers' estate is imparted by, among other things, the unplastered brick houses lining the narrow streets.

KATOWICE. "Wujek" coal m a symbol of Polish resista to martial law imposed in 19

KATOWICE. Korfantego Avenue features the Neo-Renaissance building of the Silesian Museum.

KATOWICE also boasts a three-winged Monument to the Silesian Uprisings of 1919, 1920 and 1921 which was unveiled in 1967.

...WIĘCIM, still better known...millions by its German name...uschwitz, remains a symbol...he Holocaust. The site...he former Nazi concentration...p is today a museum...lling the full horror of what...pened here.

Watchtower in Auschwitz II-Birkenau.

BRZEZINKA (Birkenau) held a sub-camp of the parent Oświęcim (Auschwitz) Concentration Camp. This is a characteristic railway loading platform.

CZĘSTOCHOWA. The miraculous likeness of the Black Madonna of Jasna Góra is an icon which has attracted millions of pilgrims down the centuries.

CZĘSTOCHOWA. The fortified Jasna Góra Monast which resisted the 17th-century inva of Poland by the Swe

CZĘSTOCHOWA. The first gate reached by pilgrims is the Lubomirski Gate erected in the years 1722-1723. It is crowned by figures of Saints Paul and Anthony, as well as the Archangel St. Michael.

LICHEŃ STARY, The Sanctuary of Mary – built with subscriptions from the faithful at the end of the 20th century – is the largest Catholic place of worship anywhere in Poland.

GÓRKA KLASZTORNA – Holy Week each year sees a famous Mystery Play put on here.

TUM, near Łęczyca, boasts a stone Romanesque collegiate church from the 12th century.

LICHEŃ STARY is a famous place of pilgrimage not far from Konin, with a Sanctuary to the Virgin Mary kept by Marian priests containing the miraculous likeness of the Licheń Mother of God.

SIERADZ. Here the Sieradzanie ensemble present the śmigus-dyngus folk custom entailing the soaking of all-comers with water on Easter Monday.

KALISZ. In a town whose history extends back to the c[...] of the Roman Empire, a modern church – of Di[...] Mercy – which was consecrated in 19[...]

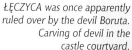

SULEJÓW. The Late Romanesque Cistercian Monastery complex with St. Thomas's Church erected from blocks of sandstone plus bricks.

SANNIKI. A neo-Renaissance palace stylised as an Italian villa. A statue of Frédéric Chopin stands in front of it.

ŁĘCZYCA was once apparently ruled over by the devil Boruta. Carving of devil in the castle courtyard.

KOŁO. The ruins of the 14th-century Gothic castle by the River Warta.

...URZYCE. The Łowicz Region Outdoor ...seum and the interior of a small house ...playing the folk-art interiors that ...ion is famous for.

SPICIMIERZ. The Corpus Christi processional route is carpeted with flowers.

...IEJÓW. The remodelled castle dating ...k to the 14th century was once ... residence of Bishops.

ŁÓDŹ is a city whose flowering came in the n
19th century, as the textile industry developed. In t
photo, Freedom Square (Plac Wolności) with its Monume
to Tadeusz Kościuszko, Church of the Holy Spirit a
former Town Hall from the 19th centu

ŁÓDŹ is rich in Old Secession-style
architecture. This is the Neo-
Baroque palace complex of the
Poznański family, with its rich
eclectic-style facade.

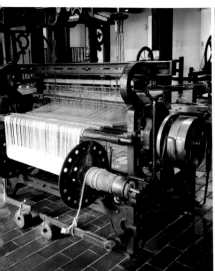

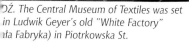
ÓDŹ. The Central Museum of Textiles was set in Ludwik Geyer's old "White Factory" (Biała Fabryka) in Piotrkowska St.

ŁÓDŹ. The Founders of Industrial Łódź is one of the statues in the open-air Gallery of Great Inhabitants of Łódź. This comprises bronze sculptures by Marcel Szytenchelm, placed along Piotrkowska St.

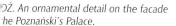
ÓDŹ. An ornamental detail on the facade of the Poznański's Palace.

ŁÓDŹ. Maurycy Poznań's Mansion, otherwise the Museum of Art. Beautiful eclectic stained glass forms a decorative element of the grand staircase.

OPORÓW. The Gothic Knights' Castle b
of brick in a square shape, surrounded
a moat and pa

NIEBORÓW – palace, containing
the painting gallery and ancient
sculpture collection founded
in the 18th century.

Łowicz folk costume characteri
of the Mazowsze regi

ŻAZOWA WOLA, the birthplace of Frédéric Chopin.
Chopin family's manor-house.

BROCHÓW boasts a Gothic-Renaissance fortified church
in which Frédéric Chopin was baptized.

WALEWICE has a Neo-Classical palace associated with
Maria Walewska, famed for her romance with Napoleon.

BOGUSZYCE.
St. Stanisław's
Church retains its
Renaissance-style
painting, not least
is likeness of Christ
on the caissoned
ceiling.

ŻYRARDÓW retains (and in a well-preserved state) its planned
layout and characteristic brick architecture from the late
19th century era of industrialisation.

TORUŃ. The Neo-Renaissance Artus Ho
dating back to the end of the 19th cent

TORUŃ. Here we see the monument to the city's
most famous son, Nicholas Copernicus, against
the background of the Gothic-style Town Hall.

TORUŃ. A model of the Cassini probe to be
seen in the Orbitarium – one of the rooms
at Toruń's Władysław Dziewulski Planetarium.

TORUŃ. This heritage-rich old town was once within
the Hanseatic League. The still-surviving Mediaeval
street layout lined by red-roofed buildings.

The arms of Toruń above the Town Hall gate.

BYDGOSZCZ. The modern "New Granary" (Nowe spichrze) development by the River Brda is recognised as an icon of contemporary architecture and is a background for the "Three Graces" sculpture.

BYDGOSZCZ, with the Statue of the Archer.

INOWROCŁAW. A Romanesque Church from the turn of the 12th and 13th centuries. It owes its present condition to reconstructions carried out in 1901 and in 1950.

CHEŁMNO is a picturesque town that retains its mediaeval town plan. Standing on a market square covering more than 1.5 ha, the 14th-century Town Hall was remodelled in the Mannerist style two centuries later.

CIECHOCINEK has been a place to spa waters since the 19th century. Here, the wooden building in which salty vapours can be inhaled,

LUBOSTROŃ. The Neo-Classical residence from the years 1795-1800 is to a Stanisław Zawadzki design and is of square plan.

GNIEW. Overlooking the Vistula is a 14th-cent[ury] castle of the Teutonic Knights that was b[uilt] in the shape of a regular squ[are.]

GOLUB-DOBRZYŃ boasts a 14th-century castle remodelled in Renaissance style in the 1600s. Each year, this plays host to tournaments of jousting and other chivalrous skills.

GOLUB-DOBRZYŃ. One of the old cannon[s] on display below the Castle.

RADZYŃ CHEŁMIŃSKI. A castle of the Teutonic Knights in the late 13th and early 14th centuries, it fell into Polish hands from 1466, through until 1772.

IDZYN has a monumental Gothic castle
rick, together with a fortified cathedral
t by the Order of the Teutonic Knights.

MALBORK – another town of the Teutonic Knights
– is situated on the bank of the Nogat. The castle,
which was the seat of the Order's Grand Masters, dates
back to the 13th-15th centuries, and is one of the finest
surviving examples of a Mediaeval fortress.

MALBORK. A Gothic-style
brick masterpiece is this
arch in one of the many
cloisters of the High Castle's
first floor.

FROMBORK. The cathedral, the most stunning of the Varmia (Ermland) churches, was built in the years 1329-1388.

FROMBORK. A module from the ceramic frieze surrounding the portal of the Cathedral.

THE IŁAWA LAKELAND is a sub-part of the Mazury region with almost 100 lakes of its own.

VARMIA, and the Buczyniec Inclined Plane along the Elbląg Canal. This was built in the mid 19th century to make transport to Elbląg more efficient.

MORĄG is a town founded in 1327 by the Teutonic Knights. Pictured here is the remodelled Gothic-style Town Hall.

GRUNWALD. The Monument to the Victors of the Battle of Grunwald commemorates the defeat of the Teutonic Knights here in 1410.

OLSZTYN on the River Łyna and wit
the Olsztyn Lakeland. This reconstruc
14th-century castle was that of
Varmia Chap

OLSZTYN. Freedom Square (Plac Wolności)
with its early 20th-century Town Hall built
in a style that recalls the Baroque
and Renaissance periods.

OLSZTYN. The Monum
to Copernicus in front of the Ca
– the great astronomer's hom
the years 1520-1521, during the
between Poland and the Teutonic Knig

LIDZBARK WARMIŃSKI – from the mid 14th century this was the seat of the Bishops of Varmia. The Gothic-style Bishop's Palace has a square design.

RESZEL. The castle of the Bishops of Varmia dating back to the mid 14th century. The 19th-century northern wing has been converted into a church.

A folk group guards the traditions of the Varmia-Mazury region.

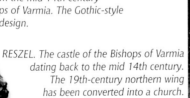

ŚWIĘTA LIPKA boasts a Baroque Jesuit monastery complex with the Church of the Visitation. The interior of the latter has a famous organ with moving decorative elements.

STAŃCZYKI. Poland's tallest viaduct carrying a now-disused railway line.

WIGRY. The Baroque-st post-Cameldolite monaste complex by Lake Wig

WIGRY. The monumental gateway leading on to the Monastery's upper terrace. The Brothers' peace is guarded by Saints Romuald and Roch, as patrons of the Camaldolese Order.

E RIVER BIEBRZA and its tributaries create extensive *odlands in spring. The National Park established here* *tects rare flora and fauna, as well as the unique natural* *dscape of the floodplain.*

KRUSZYNIANY.
Recalling 17th-century
Tartar settlement is this
wooden mosque,
which continues to
serve the local
community to
this day.

ECHANOWIEC boasts
the Outdoor Museum
of Agriculture with its
mples of peasant and
anorial buildings. This
windmill was brought
here from a village
in Podlasie region.

HAJNÓWKA. Polychromy and the iconostasis in the Orthod[ox] Church of the Holy Trinity. The work was done in 19[ ] by Greek artist Dymitrios Andonopu[ ]

BIAŁYSTOK. The Parish Church of the Assumption of Mary comprises a small Baroque-style place of worship with a Neo-Gothic Archicathedral built on to it.

BIAŁYSTOK. The Baroque Palace of the Branicki Family is situated in a large landscaped park known as the "Versailles of Podlasie".

BIAŁYSTOK. The Mansion's Baroque-style garden featu[re] stone status of, for exampl[e] a sphinx – one of two guarding the bridge on to the upper terrace.

ŁOWIEŻA NATIONAL PARK is of such importance
the world that UNESCO has recognised it as both
iosphere Reserve and a World Heritage Site.

THE BIAŁOWIEŻA FOREST
is a unique, pristine wilderness,
whose greatest attraction is probably
the European bison.

PŁOCK. Part of the bronze Płock Door dating back to the years 1152-11 and cast for Płock Cathedr

CZERWIŃSK was once a centre of trade along the Vistula. It features a monastery of canons-regular with a Romanesque church.

CZERWIŃSK. The Romanesque-style capital of a column from the church portal.

)CK. A panorama of the Tumski Heights,
‍h the Castle and Cathedral above
right bank of the Vistula.

KONSTANCIN-JEZIORNA, is a small town of
old villas and sanatoria which provides salt
inhalations in its spa-park.

LIW lies on the boundary between
the Mazovia and Podlasie regions.
Here the gate tower of the old Castle
of the Dukes of Mazovia plus
Baroque-style manor.

SIERPC. The Museum of the Mazovian
Countryside brings together old
farmsteads, chapels and farming
implements on a 60 ha site.

PUŁTUSK. The Market Square, cobbled
with stones taken from the fields,
is more than 400 m long. This makes
it the longest in Poland.

WARSAW. The Ballroom (or Great Assembly Hall) in the wing fac[ing] the Vistula, built in 1740-46. The room, designed by Domen[ico] Merlini and Jan Christian Kamsetzer, is ornamented with stat[ues] of Apollo and Minerva by André Le Brun, saved from war dama[ge].

WARSAW. Castle Square with the King Zygmunt III Waza Column – Warsaw's first secular monument, dating from 1643–4 and owing to the King's son, Władysław IV. Right – the facade of the Royal Castle.

WARSAW. The Barbican – the impressive fortification of the New Town Gate within the defensive walls of the Old Town.

WARSAW. The Old Town Market Square with tenement houses rebuilt faithfully in their 17th-18th century forms.

WARSAW. Freta Street in New Town district. On the left, St. Jacek's Church of the Dominican Order. The place of worship on the right is in turn the Pauline Order's Church of the Holy Ghost.

WARSAW. The Mermaid of the Old Town is but one representation of this aquatic symbol of Warsaw, which features on the city's coat of arms.

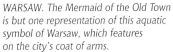

WARSAW. The Ballroom of Łazienki Park's Palace on the Island. The clean Neo-Classical lines were supplemented by sculpturework conferring a sense of antiquity, not least this 17th-century copy of the Apollo Belvedere.

WARSAW. The Łazienki Park and Palace complex with its neo-Classical Palace on the Island. This was the seat of Poland's last King, Stanisław August Poniatowski, who reigned until 1795.

WARSAW. Łazienki Park – the doorknocker of the Palace on the Island.

WARSAW. Wilanów, on the city's southern edge, boasts one of the finest magnate's residences in Poland. Here we see the front elevation of the palace, which was summer home to King Jan III Sobieski (reigning 1674-1696).

RSAW. Suspended from a single pylon,
Świętokrzyski Bridge is seen here against
overall panorama of Warsaw and the Copernicus
nce Centre by the Vistula.

WARSAW. On the site of the old
Dziesięciolecia Stadium (opened in 1955 to
mark the "10th Anniversary" of Party rule),
there has now arisen the National Stadium.

WARSAW. Monument to the Little
Upriser was erected to honour
those children who fought for
Warsaw in 1944.

WARSAW. The fifties-style Palace of Culture
and Science has become its own unique
kind of tourist attraction.

WARSAW. Supported on its reinforced concrete "le
the InterContinental Hotel incorporates that character
cut-away section to allow light through to neighbou
blocks of lesser height. The second high-rise builc
is the Warsaw Finance Cen

WARSAW. Inside the Warsaw University Library
– a modern (1999) building of interest spatially
and Architecturally, which is by Marek Budziński
and Zbigniew Badowski.

WARSAW. This undulating glass roof
covers a vast area of retail space
within the "Golden Terraces" Mall.

WARSAW. The view of a new icon of the capital – the 192-metre apartment block known as "The Sail", which was designed by Daniel Libeskind.

WARSAW. The slender forms of karyatids bear the weight of the glass Supreme Court building, which is owing to a team of architects under Marek Budzyński.

WARSAW. The Plac Wilsona Metro Station in Żoliborz is regarded as the capital's most beautiful. The elliptical dome illuminates the station in different colours, depending on the time of day.

KAZIMIERZ DOLNY – a picturesque place of recrea[tion] by the Vistula – has a Renaissance-style architectural lay[out]. This is the Market Square with a view of the parish chu[rch.]

KOZŁÓWKA. The imposing marble stairs from the late 19th and early 20th centuries with a Neo-Rococo balustrade and masterly plasterwork.

KAZIMIERZ DOLNY. An element of the Renaissance facade to the Celejowska tenement house on Senatorska Street.

NAŁĘCZÓW is a spa for the treatment of cardiac ailments thanks to its mild lowland climate and healing waters.

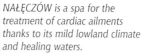

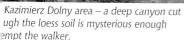
Kazimierz Dolny area – a deep canyon cut
ugh the loess soil is mysterious enough
mpt the walker.

KODEŃ. The Late-Renaissance St. Anne's
Church is a sanctuary with a miraculous
likeness of the Mother of God known as the
Queen and Mother of Podlasie.

KOSTOMŁOTY. The Orthodox Church of
St Nikita, the Sanctuary of the Uniates
of Podlasie, with a historic iconostas is
dating from the late 18th century.

LUBLIN. The interior of the Cathedral, which was once Jesuit Church of Saints John the Baptist and the Evang

LUBLIN. The view from the Trinity Tower over the roofs of the Old Town, the Krakowska Gate, the Neo-Classical-style New Town Hall and the Church of the Holy Spirit (once a hospital).

LUBLIN, Po Farze Square. The Parish Church of St. Michael was once located here. It dated back to the late 13th century, but was knocked down in the 19th. Its original foundations have been exposed.

LIN. From the 12th century onwards this was a fortified town
devastated at regular intervals by invaders from the east. The Gothic
chapel of the Holy Trinity dates from the mid 14th century,
is supported by a single column. The interiors are decorated by
unique Byzantine-Russian frescoes funded by King Władysław Jagiełło.

LUBLIN. This facade is of the 14th-century
castle rebuilt in the Neo-Gothic style at
the beginning of the 19th century.

ZAMOŚĆ. The 17th-century coat of arms of the Polish ordinate Tomasz Zamoyski

ZAMOŚĆ is a city with a unique Renaissance architectural layout and town plan. The Mannerist-Baroque style Town Hall from the 17th century features a 52-metre tower.

ZAMOŚĆ. 17th-century arcaded tenement houses on the Old Market Square recall the Renaissance architecture of Italy

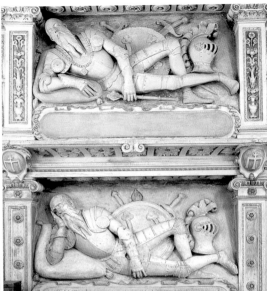

ŻAJSK is on the edge of the Sandomierz Forest.
e 17th-century organ in the town's Bernardine
rch is one of Poland's finest.

UCHANIE. In the Church of the Assumption
of the Blessed Virgin Mary we find the five-metre
tomb of Arnulf Uchański and his son Stanisław,
made of Pinczów stone.

NCUT. A Glorietta from 1800
he Castle Gardens.

ŁAŃCUT. The 17th-
century castle was
rebuilt in the style
of the French
Neo-Baroque.

73

RZESZÓW and the Castle of the Lubomirski fam
This is a 19th-century construction built up
surviving fortifications from at least 200 years earl

SANDOMIERZ is a beautiful example
of architectural and town planning.
This photograph shows the Market Square
with its Renaissance Town Hall.

JAROSŁAW is an old fortified town on the heights
above the River San. The Market Square has a
Town Hall that is now Neo-Renaissance in style.

A flower motif on the wall
of a house in the "painted
village" of ZALIPIE, where
local tradition requires
the decoration of building
and equipment alike.

BARANÓW SANDOMIERSKI boasts
a Mannerist-style 16th-17th century
castle with characteristic corner towers.

...E WESTERN BIESZCZADY MOUNTAINS. The renowned
...much-visited massif of Połonina Wetlińska, which
...ks at 1255 m Roh.

KRASICZYN features the Renaissance-
Mannerist castle of the Krasicki family set
in a 19th-century landscaped park.

THE SOLIŃSKIE RESERVOIR
was created by the damming
of the San and is a major
centre for watersports.

OWCZARY. The wooden Orthodox Church of the Care of Holy Family was built in 1653. Since 1998 this place of worsh has been the joint seat of Roman- and Greek-Catholic parish

TURZAŃSK.
The St. Michael
the Archangel Orthodox
Church which preserves
icons from 1895.

OWCZARY.
At the Orthodox Chu
one of the four cheru
painted on the dome
above the chancel.

...NÓW. This shady arcade extends out from the row ...enement houses forming the northern side of the Market ...are – as seen here from Żydowska Street.

PRZEMYŚL. Built here in the 1514-1542 period following the razing of the old Mediaeval fortress was one of Poland's first bastion-style Renaissance castles.

NOWY SĄCZ, situated in a basin, has an Eclectic late 19th-century Town Hall in the centre of its market square.

LASKOWA. A beautiful polychrome from 1677 has been preserved on the ceiling of a Baroque wooden manor house.

SZYMBARK. The fortified mansion of the Gładysz family, built in the 16th century, is now part of an open-air ethnographic museum.

UJAZD. The ruins of Krzyżtopór Castle, which w
erected by Krzysztof Ossoliński in the years 1621-16
and has lines inspired by astrolo

KRZEMIONKI. The mine for striped flint
here was first worked in the Neolithic
period, between about 3900 and 1600 BC.
The visitor to this Archaeological Reserve
can see a specifically-prepared recreation
of the work of the miner-cum-flint-knapper.

CHĘCINY. The ruins of the Royal Castle
from the late 13th and early 14th
centuries. A fine view of the
Świętokrzyskie Mountains can
be had from its restored tower.

JASKINIA RAJ — one of Poland's
most beautiful caves, it has
a wealth of stalactites
and stalagmites.

HOCK. The Cistercian Monastery funded in 1179 to this day ns some of its original structures, not least this Refectory ling with its ornate Romanesque stonework.

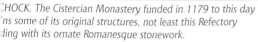

KIELCE. Dating back to 1638, this plafond in the apartment of the Palace of the Bishops of Kraków presents "The Judging of the Arians", from the studio of Tommaso Dolabella.

ŚWIĘTY KRZYŻ. East of Kielce, in the Łysa Góra Massif, is a Benedictine Abbey funded by Bolesław the Wrymouth in the 12th century.

KOŃSKIE. The Romanesque portal of St Nicholas' church is a testament to its 13th-century origins.

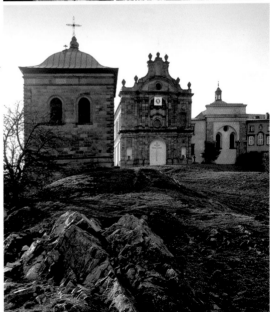

BOBOLICE. The Castle reconstructed
by private owner Jarosław W. Lasecki.

OGRODZIENIEC. The ruins of the 16th-century
Renaissance-style castle sit upon 504 m Castle Hill,
the highest point in the Kraków-Częstochowa Upland.

MIRÓW. Ruins of the Gothic-style
castle erected in the 14th century
(the times of Kazimierz the Great).

THE KRAKÓW-CZĘSTOCHOWA UPLAND is a limestone plateau on which such rocks are a characteristic element of the landscape.

PIESKOWA SKAŁA, the Renaissance-style castle. This was one of more than ten strongholds that once guarded the route leading from Cracow to the Wielkopolska region (today's Eagles' Nests Trail or Szlak Orlich Gniazd).

KRAKÓW (Cracow). The coat of arms of the
above the entrance to Samuel Maciejow
16th-century mansion in Kanonicza St

KRAKÓW. View from the tower of St. Mary's
Church towards Wawel Royal Castle.

KRAKÓW. The Wawel Hill with the C
Courtyard and its Renaiss
column-arcaded clois

KÓW. The Mariacki Church has
"tar by Veit Stoss, which was carved
ne wood in the 15th century.

KRAKÓW is a historic city, and a centre
of Polish culture and national identity.
e Main Market Square (Rynek Główny)
ith the Clothiers' Hall and Gothic-style
Church of the Virgin Mary.

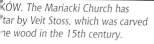

KRAKÓW. The Old Synagogue at
Szeroka Street is the oldest such place
vorship in Kazimierz, now playing host
a branch of the Historical Museum of
Cracow and its exhibition entitled
The History and Culture of the Jews.

KALWARIA ZEBRZYDOW
The Baroque Basilica of the An
Mother of God and Bernardine Monas

WIELICZKA. The underground Chapel
of St. Kinga was developed in 1896
in the old salt mine. Most of its
fixtures and sculptures are
carved out of the salt.

NOWY WIŚNICZ. The Baroque-style fortyfied resider
of the Lubomirski Family. The Castle's characteristic
silhouette with its corner towers.

...NO PODHALAŃSKIE. The wooden Church ...t. Michael the Archangel dates back ...e second half of the 15th century.

BINAROWA. A rainbow beam with the Crucifixion Scene at the Church of St. Michael the Archangel, installed around 1500. This place of worship is one of 7 forming an item on the UNESCO list of World Heritage Sites.

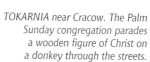

A girl in a traditional Cracovian costume.

TOKARNIA near Cracow. The Palm Sunday congregation parades a wooden figure of Christ on a donkey through the streets.

THE DUNAJEC has cut a series of bea
gorges through the Pieniny Moun
Rafting its fast-flowing waters has bed
a major tourist attrrad

NIEDZICA features a partially-ruined fort
which gained itself a fine location when
a reservoir filled behind the Czorsztyn dam.

A young raftsman
in regional costume

...KOPANE has been Poland's most famous resort ...e the 19th century. The characteristic silhouette ...iewont mountain towers above it.

ZAKOPANE. The little chapel at Jaszczurówka was designed in the Zakopianski style established by Stanisław Witkiewicz.

A girl in Highland folk costume.

THE TATRA MOUNTAINS are the loftiest and most diverse m
in the Western Carpathians. The highest peak in the Polish
of the range is 2499 m Rysy. Here we see Mnich ("The Mo
above the mountain tarn known as Morskie Oko ("The Sea's Ey

THE TATRA MOUNTAINS. At 70 metres high, Wielka
Siklawa (The Great Waterfall) in the Roztoki Valley
is the highest waterfall in Poland.

THE TATRA MOUNTAINS. Accessible to tourists,
the Mylna Cave cuts into the impressive rock
massif of Raptawicka Turnia.

THE TATRA MOUNTAINS are a mecca for Polish skiers. This is the Gąsienicowa Valley with the Granaty, Kozi Wierch, Zamarła Turnia and Kościelec peaks.

THE TATRA MOUNTAINS. The chamois is a specific element of the area's fauna.

THE TATRA MOUNTAINS. Carpets of crocuses bloom in early spring in the Chochołowska Valley.

Nicolaus Copernicus (1473-1543)

Born in Toruń, Kopernik (as he is known in Poland) went on to study in Kraków and in Italy. A multitalented man of learning, he changed thinking on Earth's place in the universe with his heliocentric theory. His work "De Revolutionibus Orbium Coelestium" ("On the Revolution of the Celestial Spheres") thus laid the foundations of modern cosmology and influenced many branches of the then scientific world.

The Monument to Nicolaus Copernicus in Warsaw was designed by Bertel Thorvaldsen.

Tadeusz Kościuszko (1746-1817)

Jan III Sobieski (1629-1696)

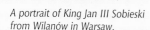

King of Poland from 1674, he "won his spurs" in battle against the Swedes, the Tartar and Cosack armies and the Turks. His greatest feat of arms came in 1683, with the defeat of the Turkish army then besieging Vienna.

A portrait of King Jan III Sobieski from Wilanów in Warsaw.

A statue of King Jan III Sobieski by Warsaw's Łazienki Park. It was unveiled in 1788.

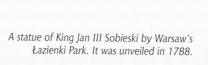

Kazimierz Pułaski (1747-1779)

Commander in the Bar Confederacy, and defender of Jasna Góra against the Russians, he commanded a cavalry brigade in George Washington's army during the American War of Independence. He died of wounds inflicted at the Battle of Savannah.

This Monument to Kazimierz Pułaski in Warka was unveiled in 1979.

...ading the armed forces during ...e so-called Kościuszko Rising of 1794, ...defeated the Russian army ...the Battle of Racławice. He had ...tinguished himself previously ...the course of the American War ...Independence, notably ...a brigadier-general at the Battle ...Saratoga in 1777.

...e Monument to Tadeusz Kościuszko ...ainst the background of the tower ...the Zymuntowska Cathedral ...the Wawel Hill in Kraków.

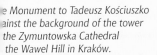

Adam Mickiewicz (1798-1855)

Poland's greatest poet, or for Poles "The Bard", he spent most of his life as an exile, for longest in France. Co-creater of the Polish Romantic Movement, ideologist and independence activist, his artistic genius can be seen in his national epic "Pan Tadeusz", amongst other places.

The Adam Mickiewicz Monument in Warsaw was funded by public contribution to mark the 100th anniversary of the author's birth.

The 18th-century palace of the Pułaski family is now the Kazimierz Pułaski Museum in Warka.

Frédéric Chopin (1810-1849))

Poland's most outstanding composer and pianist, and an icon of the Romantic era. Chopin's artistry was inspired by his country's folk music, and he composed a great many dance miniatures taking the form of waltzes, mazurkas and polonaises. His works are still among the most frequently performed. Warsaw plays host to the international piano competition held in his name every five years since 1927.

A portrait of Frédéric Chopin to be seen at his Żelazowa Wola home.

The Chopin Monument in Łazienki Park is the work of Wacław Szymanowski. Unveiled in 1926, it was deliberately destroyed during World War II, only to be faithfully reconstructed afterwards.

The first bars of Chopin's famo Polonaise in A maj

The manor house at Żelazowa Wola, the birthplace of Frédéric Chopin, is now a museum to the famous composer. Chopin piano concerts are held here regularly.

Helena Modrzejewska (1840-1909)

Poland's greatest actress, who appeared in the United States from 1877 on, under the name Modjeska. She was to play 260 roles, including 35 in English and 17 of Shakespeare's characters. She was also considered one of the outstanding beauties of her age.

Helena Modrzejewska in a picture painted by Tadeusz Adjukiewicz.

Ignacy Jan Paderewski (1860-1941)

A bust of Ignacy Jan Paderewski at the Frédéric Chopin Academy of Music in Warsaw.

Joseph Conrad (1857-1924)
(Teodor Józef Konrad Korzeniowski)

Twenty years as a mariner left Conrad, who became a British citizen in 1886, one of the greatest of all writers of sea stories. Against such a background, he placed great emphasis on matters ethical, notably honour, duty, loyalty and moral rectitude. His best-known works include "Heart of Darkness", "Almayer's Folly" and "Lord Jim".

The monument to Józef Konrad Korzeniowski (Joseph Conrad) at the very edge of the sea in Gdynia.

The outstanding pianist, composer, politician and social activist whose efforts help lead to the rebirth of the Polish state. He signed the Treaty of Versailles in 1919 as Prime Minister and Foreign Secretary of his newly-reestablished country, and went on to represent it in the League of Nations.

Maria Skłodowska-Curie (1867-1934)

A great Polish physicist and chemist living in France and married (from 1895) to French physicist Pierre Curie. Together they discovered the elements radium and polonium in 1898 – an achievement for which they won the Nobel Prize for physics in 1903. The by-then- widowed Maria went on to win a second, for chemistry, in 1911.

The Monument to Maria Skłodowska-Curie on the small square by the Warsaw Centre for Oncology bearing her name. Pre-War this was known as the Radium Institute.

Karol Szymanowski (1882-1937)

The Atma Villa was the place of Karol Szymanowski's stays in Zakopane. It is now a museum devoted to the composer's life and work

A Polish composer the "Young Poland" period whose work involved the artistic stylization of Polish folk music especially that of the Kurpie and Highland regions. His best known works include the opera "Król (King) Roger" and the ballet "Harnasie"

Józef Piłsudski (1867-1935)

A great statesman who was Naczelnik ("Leader") and Marshal of Poland. In the years 1919-20, he successfully pursued a military campaign against the Russian bolsheviks, crowning the achievement with the 1921 Peace of Riga. Five years later he staged what became known as the "May Coup". He was twice Prime Minister of his country: in 1926-28 and in 1930.

The Monument to Marshal Józef Piłsudski stands by the Belvedere Palace next to Warsaw's Łazienki Park. It was unveiled in 1998.

Jan Paweł II
(Karol Wojtyła)
(1920-2005)

Elected Pope in 1978, as the first non-Italian for 400 years. He was born in Wadowice, studied at universities in Kraków and Rome, and became Metropolitan Archbishop of Kraków in 1964. He was elevated to Cardinal in 1967. In the time that he was the Pope has made no fewer than 104 foreign pilgrimages.

e Polish Pope John Paul II, was the spiritual mainstay for his fellow
ntrymen and women in their years of struggle with
communist system, as well as in the subsequent period
ransformation in post-1990 Poland. Included among
Beatified of the Catholic Church on May 1st 2011,
d made a saint on April 27th 2014.

*A statue of John Paul II before the All Saints Church
in Warsaw's Grzybowski Square.*

Lech Wałęsa (born 1943)

Famed as a trade-union activist and politician, though an electrician by profession, Wałęsa rose to prominence as the unchallenged and unquestioned leader of Solidarity (Solidarność) – the independent trade union that emerged and grew between August 1980 and December 1981 into an independence-minded social movement of 10 million members. Things had all started with Wałęsa as one of the organisers of a localised strike at the Gdańsk Shipyard, but this and subsequent events are widely considered to have played a key role in the wave of democratic change that swept through the Eastern Bloc as a whole in the 1980s. The achievements (and what they promised) were such as to earn Wałęsa the 1983 Nobel Peace Prize. In the newly-democratic Poland of 1990, Lech Wałęsa was elected President, serving one full five-year term in that office.

On November 15th 1989, Lech Wałęsa gave his historic address before a joint session of both Houses of the US Congress.

Jerzy Owsiak in Gdańsk during the 16th (2008) Final of the "Great Orchestra of Holiday Help" (Wielka Orkiestra Świątecznej Pomocy) (Archive photo from WOŚP taken by Arek Drygas).

Jerzy Owsiak (born 1953)

Social activist, journalist, co-founder and President of the "Great Orchestra of Holiday Help" (Wielka Orkiestra Świątecznej Pomocy), which "played" for the first time in 1993. Telethon-like in structure, each year's Orkiestra collects money for the purchase of medical equipment capable of supporting health and lives among children, and lately also the elderly. By the end of the 2014 event, in excess of 200 million US dollars had been raised. The actions are followed and participated in enthusiastically by the Polish public each year, and this vast charitable undertaking does much to promote the good name of Poland far and wide. Owsiak's Foundation is also behind rock concerts under the Przystanek Woodstock title, bringing young people together in the name of "Love, Friendship and Music", as well as commitments to eschew violence and narcotics.